I0880154

Praise for *Cajun South Brown Folk*:

"In *Cajun South Brown Folk,* Shome Dasgupta's well-crafted poems traverse East Indian culture via Louisiana's Lafayette Cajun home base. These poems tell stories in Louisiana English interspersed with Bengali, or its endonym Bangla, a classical Indo-Aryan language from the Indo-European language family native to the West Bengal of India. Readers are at once transported from Cajun Lafayette life to Indian family ties, and the two cultures kiss us warmly in memorable verse. From a 'Cajun espresso sunrise' and crawfish seasons of Acadiana to khichuri, or rice and beans of Indian cuisine, thank you Shome Dasgupta, for this unique gift."

—Mona Lisa Saloy, author of *Black Creole Chronicles,*
and Poet Laureate of Louisiana, 2021-2023

"When you read Shome Dasgupta's *Cajun South Brown Folk*, it feels like you're watching two movies simultaneously, one recorded over the other but failing to erase the original in its entirety. Through Dasgupta's 'cut and splice,' we are lulled into a cinematic game of comparison, one in which we are prompted to find the similarities between two places by sifting through their differences. We jump from Kolkata to Acadiana, from a Bengali kitchen to a Cajun one, from the speaker's mother's wrists to his own, and through these leaps we begin to see a cultural common denominator of deep love, both familial and communal. These are poems that know something about tenderness, that know that love is in the field, the kitchen, the food, the hand."

—Taylor Byas, author of *I Done Clicked My Heels Three Times*

Praise for Shome Dasgupta:

"There's so much tenderness in these stories, all wrapped in vibrantly bubbling scenes and conversations. Dasgupta cares about all these characters and it shows all over the pages and pulls a reader in."

—Aimee Bender

"Page by page, these stories transport, restore, nourish, and remind. They bring us chocolates and curries, mud and family, songs and sights from all over the planet. More than anything, they show us humanity. And for that, for this author, I am truly grateful."

—Jack B. Bedell, Poet Laureate of Louisiana, 2017–2019

Cajun South Brown Folk

BELLE POINT PRESS
Fort Smith, Arkansas

Cajun South Brown Folk

poems

Shome Dasgupta

CAJUN SOUTH BROWN FOLK

Cover image: *Le Lapin*, Catherine Fontenot

Edited by Casie Dodd
Design & typography by Belle Point Press

Belle Point Press, LLC
Fort Smith, Arkansas
bellepointpress.com
editor@bellepointpress.com

Find Belle Point Press
on Facebook, Substack,
and Instagram (@bellepointpress)

Printed in the United States of America

29 28 27 26 25   1 2 3 4 5

Library of Congress Control Number: 2025946458

ISBN: 978-1-960215-47-5

CSBF/BPP50

for Heidi

Contents

Only the Cow Knew

Windblown erosion—at the intersection
of two dirt roads where bales of hay
once played with wrens and robins.
One street sign, nodding over
like my baro dadu at the kitchen table
when we ate maach and aloo bhaji, tired and quiet.
I was just a brat visiting family in Kolkata,
wanting to go back to Lafayette for driveway
basketball and cable TV—air conditioners and soft beds.

Heading down this crumpled road
to pick up crawfish and corn, I remember his thick
dark-framed glasses and neatly parted hair—
thin and combed and shiny, wearing a V-neck white T-shirt
with a baggy dhoti—a silent gentleman with creased eyes.

He was in the Korean War, or maybe Vietnam—
these were stories I never heard. On that afternoon
in my mejo dadu's flat, my great uncle said in a light
voice, "Oh right. I think so. Today might be my birthday—
I think I remember now." I remember now.

He spoke to himself more than anyone else, in frail
Bangla—like he found a gem in his mind, once forgotten
for years—hidden in dirt. How on that afternoon—
as a cow's bell rocked lazily from afar, its song
coming through the balcony rails—for the first time,
I realized my own selfish nature, embarrassed.

A hug was never enough, but there was laughter
—one I hadn't heard before. Maybe, it was a good day.
Maybe, candles and cake weren't needed—just a memory.
Six pounds of boiled crawfish and a few potatoes and corn
on the cobs for me and Mom—driving back to the house,
I can't help but to wonder, what image did he see
when he remembered that it was the day he was born.

A Louisiana Sestina

Layered mists over dewed green grass fields—a Cajun espresso sunrise,
a rooster sings from across the pond where minnows tend to their ripples.
Stubborn hay bales and rusted tractors make a palace for a whiskered rabbit,
and a tilted barn—stripped and ripped—with unhinged doors, emits a history
of chickens and horses and barefoot shovels. A wooden rocking chair, still—
chipped and toothless, waits for a familiar snout to rest upon its split skin.

Dirt and pebbles—glittered glass, stained with holy paint, a shine. Its skin
shimmers, casting gleam and light upon a terrain echoing under the sunrise.
Cowbells: wind chime, lulling a sleep to find a blanket of blades, soft and still.
A whisper of fried green tomatoes—a gumbo on the horizon, its scent ripples,
sauntering in like humid mosquitoes on a summer night full of a fabled history.
Dandelion dreams sprinkle a manured air—Gulf winds raise ears of a rabbit.

A solo Eastern Phoebe perches on a branch, in conversation with a rabbit.
The language of nature where no translation is needed—a kindred of skin.
Cayenne and jalapeño peppers sprouting, they know the tongue's history,
and how the evenings disappear and blend into the dawn's hues of a sunrise
—a bayou born to plant its southern seeds. Dispersed through zydeco ripples,
a Vermilion threads a blanket for crawfish ponds and rice fields—never still.

Rustic trucks blooming with sugar cane—a harvest moon, teardrops still
falling from the sky until the ashes flitter away onto the nose of a rabbit.
Magnolia trees and oak-carved canoes find reflections in a pond's ripples,
a rested turtle upon the banks swivels its head—darting pecans, hard skin
meets its mirror, a shell for a shell, and a pelican floats below the sunrise.
Caked acres and irrigated soil continue to replenish its own fertilized history.

You—once a ghost, a myth, creating your own rougarou in a flooded history.
Now alive, in peace with river palettes—a spectral hazed statue standing still
among electric wires and power surges. Perhaps, one winter, a cold sunrise
when you evaporated into my mind, fiery and furious, leaving a field rabbit
to nibble on your remnants and debris. A rural Sistine Chapel of folklore skin,
where we danced in sunflower ant piles—castles of reverberations and ripples.

I'm sitting here this morning, marinating—
        we were a story never read, that ripples
down the Atchafalaya stemming from our hands
        and how they once held a history.
Soon, a moss-filled moon—I'm at the dinner table
        eating alone, remembering skin
and a peach to quench a spiced throat full
        of a Louisiana red. Keep memories still
I whisper to a plain of dawn's horizon and sit back
        and extend a palm to a rabbit,
your only mirage while an armadillo licks its paws
        and scutters away to the sunrise.

A hen's laughter ripples from beyond a fog, and my friend—a deer stands still,
a glance and a nod, she lets me know our history lives
        in the eyes of the rabbit.
I rub the goosebumps on my skin and listen
        to the twilight waltz of the sunrise.

A Rabbit Under the Sun

Pollen-covered windshield—
streaked with humidity,
slashes of the sun perforated
a milky way. Through holes:

a rabbit and raised ears.
A quick shift to a Bengali
street kitten stretched
on a plain of a cow, stood

before rubble and litter.
Orange peels and mango
skins—dew drenched
bananas. They looked sad.

Kolkata feasts or firewood,
such rich blessings of streets.
Gentle scratches and claws
of comfort, a home of smog

and smoke. Back: Acadiana
—down the road, scrunched
eyes and squinted jaws molded,
a rabbit under the sun—a mirage

for a crumpled Popeyes bag
full of fries and crumbled
grease, perhaps—hunched
and wilted, on asphalt fields.

Down Smede Road

Pecan pie: once Ma peeled a mango, showing how sunlight saunters in through the balcony rails on a rusty Kolkata morning. I was twelve then, the skin—its complexion matched her mama's walking stick: her uncle—the oil in his hair made me want to be proper. Proper—back in Lafayette, under a Louisiana rouge, I foiled my first attempt at baking: gathered pecans under tall speechless bark where sugar cane fields patched the earth, tall enough for hide and seek. Ziploc bags pierced and shredded—I could hear them cackling, at me. October winds and ashy glittered skies: a harvest moon lullaby told me to go back to sleep. Back. The juice—its juice, the soul of Bengali tongue: rivers down the wrists until a quick lick left a sticky scent of every plucked tree in Golf Green where my grandfather lived. My Dadu was alive then—Dida, her bright red bindi and green sari spoke for her as she sat in her wheelchair: a smile and a cough. Her daughter's hand just below the mouth—hinting for a tilt of the head— hinting toward childhood days of aloo bhaji and cauliflower on aluminum. "This is how you chew the seed," Ma said, holding the sun's core between her thumb and index. Its strands—the seed's rays—flossing the teeth, a chin of yolk and gleam. One day I'll make the perfect pecan pie—one day I'll memorize its recipe without looking for ingredients: now, though—just for now, I'll keep this one on the kitchen counter to remind me of the first time I noticed the sun in India and how it sang about a family tucked away in a Kolkata winter, fresh of laundry and loss.

The Lost Saris of Crawfish Season

The scent of my mother's perfume
pressed between forgotten saris
hanging in the closet of the spare
room where my bhai once lived
before he left for Portland, Seattle,
Los Angeles, and Seattle again—
the walls—covered with chipped
paint and exposed white primer.

Every now and then, when I'm alone
and lonely, they look like a pink sky
full of clouds, reminding me of a visit
to Vienna where we ate ice cream
amid ducks and a mint chocolate
chip lake (outside, drills and hammers
banter as the Cajun fencing company
rebuilds the wood of the backyard).

I open the doors to draped cloth
full of colors and aroma—Ma's
skin against my cheek. I'm sure tears
blanket a face now full of sparkles
and glitter. We would sit in the kitchen
and peel crawfish tails—that red
fragrance of extra spicy peppered
shells with corn and potatoes.

She always tried to give me the big ones
—I'd toss them back as my own heap,
dripped upon by my own sweat, was a sign
of satisfaction. Maybe one day my brother
will join us—maybe one day there will be
15 lbs. instead of 10. For now—I'll sink
my face between the saris on the wire
hangers and lose myself in an empty room.

Us Cajun South Brown Folk

Two-steppin' Brown folk,
Creole Lunch House Brown folk,
Bindi laughin' Brown folk
    —gathering 'round the sun
    holding hands in circles,
    we stick our tongues
    out toward the mud and clay.
Muthafuckin' Brown folk,
Brown-skinned Brown folk,
Black-skinned Brown folk
    —zydeco rattlin', moon-filled music,
    red eyes and clanking bangle
    bracelets with nose-pierced, gold-silver
    shine, we celebrate our ankles.
Dem's my cousins Brown folk,
Acadiana Girard Park Brown folk,
Gumbo-sippin', masala Brown folk
    —tin-cupped palms like branches
    around the wings of an owl, our dance
    of the peacock, we look into the Mississippi
    and see the reflection of the Ganges.
Okra- and daal-bathed Brown folk,
Aloo and fish fry Brown folk,
UL Lafayette Brown folk
    —we look at each other like we know each other,
    never saying a word, maybe just a nod,
    maybe a glance, we speak in motherland
    talk, a way to shake hands—a namaste.
Atchafalaya Basin Brown folk,
Lake Martin sunset Brown folk,
Bhagavad Gita temple Brown folk

—Diwali children cracking pecans in green fields
while sari aunties hunt snakes with shovels,
frogs hiccup stories about the pond's history,
under parking lot lights, we play cricket with untucked shirts.
Sangeet-singin' Brown folk,
Do-si-do dosa Brown folk,
Tabla-tappin' Brown folk,
Puja and Sanskrit Brown folk,
Festival International de Louisiane Brown folk,
Crawfish-peelin', canoe-paddlin' Brown folk
—us Cajun South Brown folk.

Soft Marble Dirt

Sunlight lathered—rinsed in moss and moon:
childhood nights of firefly frenzies, backyard
lemonade and hummed-bird chimes, swung
where hopscotch friends learned to count
and jump. Dreams made in chalk—lawn
filled pecans: Bon Jovi radio and a rickety
single porch fan rocking in every direction,
wanting to be set free. We lived on prayer
—hoping that when the day ended, a day
will begin between two horizons, slightly
slanted: tilted to balance our thoughts.
Who knew? Years from then—lessons
from the tail of a squirrel and an owl's call
heard between each bounce of a jump
rope would lead to one gray evening—
in solitude amid a hurricane tantrum,
tied to itself, stubborn and slow. Sandbag
forts and wooden windows—we huddled
together in the whirl of the eye, clay striations,
closed our own to imagine when we counted
carrot flowers—soft marbles pressed
in our palms. Hands now clasped—gated
and firm, a tremored roof and the clack
clack clack of weathered brick and metal:
without electricity, we whistled our songs
in the dark: perhaps, one memory we speak
—of when we stuck grass between our teeth
to taste the earth and wonder about minerals.

Mel's Diner

Early Bird Special: Charlie Parker—
on the jukebox summer sweat tunes,
a memory amid the notes, noted.
This was when I drank—drunk, drink.
Clack clack ice—click clack counter:
sober now—sober you, still sober.
Once—one time, a morning walk
down dirt pebble streets of Kolkata,
where stray dogs mother kitten teeth
—blackbirds and cracked satellites,
a conch sings like waves sliding
onto my gritty tongue, a fog-filled
sun. I hear that ringing in my ribs.

Cut and splice: now.

Acadiana rains—a music patters
against the windowsills paned
to my mind: how a silent owl sits
in my garage—my Dida's red lips
and thin bangles strolling down
her wrists. I listen to ragas and blues
—no more ice and no more counters:
only a brief breeze bringing India
to my Cajun plates. A saxophone
—every now and then, chimes
in to remind me: the music remains
the same—the history of rivers
navigates new paths in chirps and dew.

Morning Raga

I've heard through stories
about my ancestors—
they told—a petal can sing
a song from before existence—
now as I look upon time
and see a rhythm—a melody,
I listen to a voice, a voice born
from a petal, one no longer
here—living before us,
after we forget our past

A Slight Resonance and Reflection

I saw no storm—that, which stirred a clatter
of bones and stems, up from unrooted days
in skies of plains where families gathered
and harmonized pain and triumph—in skies
of plains where wolves and crows laughed
in madness about trivial natures of precipitation,
a bird and a bird huddled around a rain—
each beat of a drop vibrated inside glass earths.

When a world wrestled with its own kin
and feathers from ancient veins fluttered
among present skin and tissue—where puffed
chests of tides arose upon a land thirsting
for a simple caress, a touch—this, a time of nails
and tin—a forest of heavy leaves, deluged
with sounds of evocation, an echo into hollowed
mouths carved with our own axes, axes once held
by streams of our own, a measure and meter—
we saw our chimes pat softly against a wind so silent.

I saw no storm—I'd rather none, at sea
or shore or in my mind where once a farm tilted
just a bit, a head lived like stubborn horizons
where layered clouds breathed into our past—
gave rhythm to our tongues in search of teeth,
to clasp upon and remember a cow grazing alone,
overhead a sun—perhaps our own—shifted,
a glance: a roof with no house—a house and a storm.

Acadiana Rickshaws

Rickshaw runners—their dhotis, like parachutes used for navigation, flapped against the Kolkata heat, and I sat there in a machine with an air conditioner, almost embarrassed, and looked at their calves, held up by thin sandals—thin like they're the streets themselves. There was a black cow amid the smog full of honks and dirt—unbothered by the crow on its back, pecking away with a bright yellow beak. At a light—just ahead of me, a large metal construction pipe on its side where inside were two children, one taking care of the other—the other much younger, wrapped in cloth. No faces—all holiness. There was the sun. I took a picture to capture the beauty of silence amid all the shouting engines, like driving under a canopy of oaks while it's raining. That was twenty years ago—I don't have that photo anymore, but I think about that moment every time I'm at a red light here in Acadiana. I was on my way to pick up a bowl of gumbo and a po'boy for my own pleasure, once—or many times. How lucky I am—so spoiled and fortunate. I'll never see those two again, but I meet them every day, in my mind. It's quiet now here—just a gentle hum of cars in unison—a humming that brings me back to them. There was no world to them—they were the earth. I bought the gumbo—I took home the sandwich, but I ate neither of them. I put them just out on the street in front of my house, an offering, perhaps—to a memory.

Tiresias up the Bayou

That's them opossums down there
—that's them right there, pointing
like there was someone sitting next
to him. There was no one—he talks,
a bucket of pecans: bright and yellow,
shining its transparency under a sun.

That's them opossums down there
—they know the earth like they
created the map for all geographies.
Squinted eyes—hard skin and rough,
he pushes a potato in his mouth.
Chew: blistered lip—fingertips
with no nails, a straw hat full of twilit
echoes. Echoes singing the beams
stemmed from sky's mouth—a mouth.

Down there: that's them opossums
huddling around a patch of cabbage,
making dinner for a home—recognizing
a new visitor to enter soon, and just up
there, a man with no eyes buries himself
to sleep, as if he was never awake or
awoken or there—that's the bayou.

Two Dinner Tables

Luchi and aloo: cauliflower yellow
tipped fingers and scraped plates
next to room-temperature water—
in a Louisiana home their tongues
lick the memories of a Kolkata
kitchen. Looking at my parents—
the movements of their wrists,
rhythmic and casual while I
tear my bread using two hands—
breathing hard through my nostrils.

A Day Dripped Day

Coooooooo-eeeeeeee!
Keeyaut. Keeyaut keeyaut
keeyaut. Coooo!
Sun-bled,
bleeding—a dripped day,
sky
scarred over hay baled
field, bronze and lazy, lolli-
popped green-less grass,
we lay under a canopy
of clouds
—your cousin,
killed by a bus
in Kolkata
years ago,
so a rooster's
crow echoed
—the beat
of a triangle, its tinging in our heads,
like the glint
of the sun
passing horizons of branches,
we shout the language
of the farm—much like when your cousin,
with two mangoes,
whispered
to goru, and we held hands,
our tongues waiting for fruit
and doi.

Coooooo-eeeeee.

Keeyaut. Keeyaut keeyaut

Keeyaut. Keeyaut. Coooo—

we sigh, letting the heat

sprinkle its skin on our faces.

An Ocean Between Markets

Gariahat—Ma bargained her best: eta, she pointed. Oita, she pointed—koto? An experienced index finger, one I've seen before when bhai and I were in trouble. That was how I learned Bengali best, cursing strangers and relatives for practice. Her usual nodded head, feigning to walk away before being asked to return. Na, she'd say with a quick and stern voice, pretending, moving to the next table. We'd make our rounds, bangles, tin cups, and mounds of shawls—the scent of fish roamed and sauntered—tugging Ma's hand at the bright lights of colorful toys and games. Soon, we'd be back at that table, our hands full of brown paper shopping bags, full and stuffed: koto? A pause. Haa, she'd say, tilting her head in agreement. Now, past the ocean: at the Lafayette Farmers Market, jarred honey, pecans—watercolors and plates, fresh cracklin. Saturday mornings, walking from table to table, thinking about Kolkata in December when I learned the craft of buying saris and purses while holding my mother's hand, lost in language.

The Dance of the Wayfarer

Under a fresh beam of moon, a broken root, severed and twisted—a frozen
echo waiting
screaming to be released. To be heard in a thickness of ice, a
suffocation—far from chiseled
bark—far from seeking arms.

Let shimmer the glazed lake—thin plated, perfect in silence, to break
through and crack
the surface to feel the rush of frightened earth in search for a way
to let go and forget all
restraints.

Song: a gate,
gatekeeper—escape
—go and sing
about a pebble
once heard crying
for its world.

Why did love exist—an ant, a petal, a drop of rain—they knew
an answer once, when
marbled time clinked and clanked against constellations ghostly
dreams radiating from
unseen oceans.

A winding wind—entered,
swept, an air eroded, weeping
for soil and leaves.
A soul a soul a soul—
taken amid broken fire.

Come moon—give life again, once a brittle seed found again
          in a swaying home,
planted and firm. There was no ending, only a growing core—
          a yearning, recognition of a
beginning, knowing there was more to imagine, let imagine.

Evening Like Dawn

Morning beignets—there's a glint of the sun,
and a horse, shining a hint of the sun.

An evening cold brew mocha: extra ice
—a wise hen, she is a tint of the sun.

Silent songs to breathe, a memory stands.
Kolkata ragas—they're flints of the sun.

A soporific thunder turns and sighs,
and ancestors offer lints of the sun.

Lafayette, India where Shza lives—
two worlds, he's seeking a splint of the sun.

Ladders

Sun—suppliant. Folded skies,
a swallow: mirrored creeks,
trailing—drifting, forever
a mashing, mashed—fists
of bark, scratched and scarred
like beaks of melee—like eyes
full of mud, stung from powdered
stones.

Juxtaposed: craved teeth, snarled brow—
a puff and a pout, such were the memories
of glass and dew—of patched mounds
tied by clasped grass, fingers crossed—
a crossing among sticks of light, like
hypnotic grazes of skin and bone, a release.

Pebble for pebble—a toss and a skip,
a broken roof made way for a charm,
floating—bumping—a ray of shadow
for tongues to find the path, a path—
wayward fallen upon knees, thin
and pressed—one leaf or two, feathered
like a rooster's crow—so let it be gone—
so let our failures dwindle in our palms
as those who stagger and find bits
of rope to climb until we look down
and see the dirt of our wrists.

Kolkata Crawfish Claws

Good Lo'—good Lo': good Lo'.
Awww now looky look that—
looky that: good Lo', good Lo'
—good Lo'. Now look that—
looky look: good Lo', look
looky that. Good Lo': awww,
now what we gonna do—
what we gonna do now
when no one is around, like
look look that, good Lo'. Now
what we gonna do now then?

Krishna please—Krishna please,
let light let light protect us all
now that we down here in a ditch
full of banana peels and mango
skin—Krishna please: Krishna
please, no moon to cry, looky
look that—no moon to cry now,
Good Lo', good Lo', good Lo'.

Take me back—take me back,
Good Lo': good Lo', good Lo',
take me back, take me back
to the moss and crawfish, please
Krishna—take me back to moonlit
moss and claws red like tandoori
curry, soft and savory. Good Lo',
tender like spice and throat, looky
look that now, awww looky look
Good Lo'—there floats on farm

ponds and river gleams, like Bengal
Bay fish slipping through fingers,
sliced by shell and chingri maach.

Let's go—let's go: let's go, back
home, good Lo', let go. I'm gonna
go when no one is around to see
the light like light lit near a sun,
singing Bistirna Dupare—sewing
a soul knit knotted for you. Good Lo'
—look looky that, awww now good
Lo', good Lo': good Lo'. Good Lo'.

Mawmaw

Mawmaw is no longer dead—
so says the city of Maurice:
I was at the local grocery store,
located inside the gas station,
two cans of dip at the counter—
Rooster—I needed a burn. Sore
gums and spotted teeth—black
and grainy: spitting gave purpose
to a summer Louisiana heat, rain
and Gulf humidity—nothing else
to do outside. The lady shook
her head and prayed out loud:
three Hail Marys as if the priest
is on the other side at church—
she couldn't believe it: Mawmaw
is back—she ain't dead no more.

My Dida is an owl: a visit, stooped
in our garage—she passed away
two weeks before then, Parkinson's
led her to a life of wings and wisdom.
I waved to her before she flew away,
a prayer, much like the lady behind
the counter—I saw her green sari
and bright red bindi, bangles on thin
wrists and standing on the balcony
of a Kolkata flat: yellow rusted rails
and a blackbird. The sun was special
that day, how she rose from her chair

and smiled—the bird cawed before
taking off. The owl soars into mind
today while she whispers Mawmaw:
a bird outside—I nod, maybe wave.

Soaked in Lightning

Saturation: bleached sky—
splotched splintered split,
a flash—darted fox, silver
gleam and tilted head, over
a yawn of the sun, layered—
cascaded and covered, a breath
of metallic tips, a singe,
a touch—a mane of earth
tugged and tightened.

Maze—river throats:
hollow stomachs carved
from wolf teeth, muddied
wolves, worldly wolves,
wolves of stone and moon—
an oxbow meander, stream shift
and shot light covered shine,
so a face, a face like breath
over porous foliage: peering.

Ending—an ending: sound—
a tectonic of foliage, gathered
bark, towered and tipped, a trace:
speckled histories of hand
in hand, where no one saw
silent creations of skin—
palm and chin and wrist,
you were once there, you,
you—with closed eyes:
I was once there, there,
with you when air departed
and struck us into nothing.

Abecedarian for the Sacred Roux

Allons. Grazing bald cypress bark with open palms,
bayou bends and whirring airboats full of swamp:
Cajun mornings sprinkled with mallard sunshine beaks,
Dimanche dirt prayers—andouille pews carved from fallen
elms and glass stained with sacred roux, debris and silt
filter through our pores, letting us suck in sediments.
Gumbo-burnt deltas remind us of Ganges ancestry, a
habitation where me and bhai dip our pining fingers
into the throats of our late relatives: their watery eyes
journey along the river, telling us stories about their
Kolkatan genealogy. Mythological—like rougarou tongues,
lore of folk and tale, turtle shell conchs chiming games of
mère may I: dozing gators along the banks snore and bell.
Nous—nous, we walk to Gariahat in search of onions and
okra to build castles in the kitchen with Ma and Baba. Back:
papillon pecans cocooned and covered—moon-stringed moss.
Qu'est-ce que c'est? C'est tout. Amra—me and older bhai
ride a pirogue and paddle toward a star singing our names:
siffler—ragas and talas, hypnotized from mosquito hums.
Tabla beats drum our ears from centuries ago—Dajii's
urn, a cremation to remember a kiss on the forehead:
vas, meandering amid accordion notes, floating up and up,
we fill our chests with past monsoons and marigolds, and
xylophones ring and dance from dawn's distance where les
yeaux of twilight melodies envelop like fog and mist and
zydeco clefs hover in our stomachs—a fifolet on the horizon.

Descendants

Crawfish—up 2%, five pounds
    a fortune: savor the pull and twist,
    an onion or two with a sauce
    full of garlic and horseradish.

Nostrils flexed—fingertip nicks:
    a burn and a sweat and a huff
    under a large cranky ceiling fan,
    wiping tears on red-and-white cloths.

Tedious—Baba says, watching us,
    eating gumbo with bread: corn
    cob on the side, fiery yellow.
    A catahoula sleeps outside.

At home—Ma is the expert:
    shuffling fishbones with her tongue,
    spitting them out like chewing
    tobacco. I use my hands and squint.

Years later—later, I find a memory
    in a crooked kitchen drawer:
    a recipe book of Cajun cuisine,
    next to her own notes for a curry.

Just a Bit

Amid a sunset—embedded in silence
and gleam as the world becomes soft
in its darkness—as the world
becomes a blanket and I shift my body
this way and that to gain a stronger
understanding of myself and you
so that we can soften the world, just a bit—
such as a middle of a winter sunset.

Early, the nights and days—so hand in hand
let's wander forth into blinding days
and let us lift our chins, just a bit,
to let the sky welcome us into a moment of light—
a moment to carve out of marble
and we can settle into the dirt and soil,
still and quiet and still until we are overwhelmed
with evening songs—until our hands
feel like petals sprinkled with frozen dew.

A Kolkatan Uncle Duplex

Litchi juiced like drips from a chin to a wrist.
Dirt and blood grind in the teeth of jealous eyes.

A mouth full of red dirt and blood grinds on fruit.
On golden grass, sliced mango spreads like a crown.

A mango sun rains on a golden grass green:
Uncle, prostrated and sobbing in the shine.

Uncle, in the shine of sobbing, prostrated.
He held my hand once, crossing the street for sweets.

Cakes and sweets, I held his hand to cross the street
—Uncle lives there now with ragged cloth and knees.

My uncle lives with torn knees and ragged cloth,
I'm here now in the Cajun South, soft singing:

I'm singing in the Cajun South about him—
litchi juiced like drips from a chin to a wrist.

Constellations 1: Broken French

Je pense—je pense, je pense.
Qu'est-ce que c'est? Tes yeux,
comme le soleil ou la lune—tings
from a triangle quand the evening
arrives. Il est cinq heures et je suis
sitting sur the porch avec un verre
de limonade ici en Lafayette—my
thoughts float from star to star.

Constellations 2: Bengali Broke

Tumi kemon achho? Tumi kothai?
I think about the time we laughed,
forgetting about the tears given for
a lost friend—amra tin jon natcham,
bala and bindi, tabla beats, Kolkatar
mashari nets draped like capes—
amra flew with blackbirds and swam
in the Ganga—holy and burnt.
No prithibi for us, just a moment
marbled and carved with tongues.

Constellations 3: Satellite English

I'm alone—watching a butterfly
fall asleep between two leaves.
Who am I? A reflection of dreams
found in a pond full of frogs and fish.
Somewhere near, you two, waving
and holding hands, singing to me
a song we once heard in twilight.
We played in fields, now in a mouth
of a Cajun rabbit or in sonic waves
of a Kolkata flat satellite. Let's wander
and wander among constellations—
until the mango skies root our minds.

The Clasp of the Rake

A sift of flaked leaves
and fallen moss—dirt
cooled between fingers,
crisp and brown, netted
grass itch for an earth:

slushed Louisiana under
afghans of caked foliage,
spark—a sparkle, a frail
fall and tangs of smoke
from burnt fields of cane,

teardrop ash, a flailing—
flickering like dropped
stars in horizon winds
from the Gulf. Soon—
a gathering of soft mud:

a harvest when rabbits
and raccoons lift paws
and hinds and stretch
toward evening yawn,
over a plain, a mosquito

—full, a history of farm
and thinned plains, floats
from bent petal to petal,
in search of roots, to tell
stories of times before—.

Mist over Meadow

My shona atmiya was dead once—my dida's side:
"I don't want to see the century," he told my baba.
At 99, he refused clocks—there was tea and grapes.
I remember tossing sugar cubes in my small mouth.
Mango and kiwi presented by a servant in red sari—
my first love, perhaps: aphrodisiacs—pierced nose
and jingled anklet. At home—Louisiana, a summer
Lafayette deluge: one magnolia petal floated down
the river road, and he was gone. I heard and carried
sandbags to the back porch door, looking for ripples.
The ashes of a burning Ganges, again he was alive,
perhaps to his scorn. Dawn—looking beyond a mist
over meadow, I saw his wide eyes under dazed sun.
A bird: under a flap of the wing—his twilit presence,
holding a cane. Even narrowed ghosts age in worlds
where time petrifies in hollowed stomachs, swirled.
A throat full of starlings and beaks—a gentle wave
of the hand as he walked: hunched over with a bent
back. "Shona," he spoke—a voice full of dew drops:
golden fields. A palm against my cheek and cradled
on his lap—a spirit of skin. My burnt black chicory
coffee tasted like coconut water, munching pralines
glazed—Cajun breakfasts: scents of papaya; gelled
hair—thinned. Corn grits and Indian tongues: was I
the specter, I wondered, drifting toward a confusing
horizon, pink—a rooster's call and skunk's perfume.
Another winged flap and there was no bird: a ghost
knows not its own existence unless its papered hand
touches what it felt one century ago, a mother's wrist.

Kitchen Pantoum

Feels antediluvian—Savoie's roux burns on the stove alongside a pot
of debris, simmering and sauntering.
Outside, a flood rises, maybe to erode memories embedded in our earth—
we tend to a garden of dirt and pebbles.
Ma patiently waits for the electricity to shock and shut and talks of
blackouts in Kolkata to lessen the surge.
Waves of oceanic heat remind Baba of the Bay of Bengal and how a swoosh
of air brings in tides of cremated stars.

Outside, a flood rises, maybe to erode memories embedded in our earth—
we tend to a garden of dirt and pebbles.
A heron in the rain—rather, for every flap toward a steeple to rest a beak
and listen to thunderous songs of the Gulf.
Waves of oceanic heat remind Baba of the Bay of Bengal and how a swoosh
of air brings in tides of cremated stars.
I've heard of solar storms and mathematics and stories that broken abacuses
bead away from rod to rod while Dadu and Dida sip tea in the dark.

A heron in the rain—rather, for every flap toward a steeple to rest a beak
and listen to thunderous songs of the Gulf.
Anthropomorphic clouds—magnetic and flared, a Muppets bedsheet from
childhood continues to cover my dreams where I visited relatives in
Jodhpur Park.
I've heard of solar storms and mathematics and stories that broken abacuses
bead away from rod to rod while Dadu and Dida sip tea in the dark.
Playing cricket in a back alley, bird stained and cobbled—we perfect laughter
while aunties dressed in flowery saris listen to my Thomani's voice
on vinyl.

Anthropomorphic clouds—magnetic and flared, a Muppets bedsheet from
childhood continues to cover my dreams where I visited relatives in
Jodhpur Park.
Feels antediluvian—Savoie's roux burns on the stove alongside a pot
of debris, simmering and sauntering.
Playing cricket in a back alley, bird stained and cobbled—we perfect laughter
while aunties dressed in flowery saris listen to my Thomani's voice on vinyl.
Ma patiently waits for the electricity to shock and shut and talks of
blackouts in Kolkata to lessen the surge.

The Corner Table of the World

Darrell's Famous Po'boys—the special,
it's the jalapeño mayonnaise and gravy
that makes me look around the world
with an open mouth. The Surf & Turf,
too—butter sauce and a messy chin:
Lake Charles, Louisiana—70605,
swirling palates to understand the birth
of a sandwich and its New Orleans 19th
century history beginning with fried oysters.
When the storm came, such a city beaten
and thrashed, metallic covers and splintered
woods—crumbled bricks and dented gas
stations: shattered and busted windows
and lives, I hoped our neighbors pulled
through as they always do, over and over,
to live with such obstinance is a must. A few
weeks later, my friend sent a photo—a perfect
photo of the menu from Darrell's: it's still there,
and I relished the idea that the community
still has a home to gather and laugh and taste,
to forget. A future visit I anticipate:
it's the jalapeño mayonnaise and gravy
that makes me look around the world
with an open mouth—a wandering tongue.

Seasons of the Mind

Baba sits in the living room
listening to his mother on vinyl:
she was a singer who lived
on Theatre Road in Kolkata,
my Thomani. I remember:

sweets and cakes and kisses,
scented saris and soft skin.
A voice and a rhythm: vibrant,
making me feel confused
about emotions—either way,
a constant movement. Head
rocking as when I was once
in her lap. I watch my dad—
one finger tapping his knee,
his face toward the ceiling:

how many memories birthed
from this record? He left India
for university—a career here
in Lafayette, LA: my upbringing.
Such odds? Similar spices
and seasonings. The seasons
of his mind: what if he stayed?
I would be more Indian Indian:

speaking fluent Bengali, read
and write, the nuance: hands
and heads, the subtle changes
in tones. Maybe cricket instead
of basketball: vegan or vegetarian
instead of fried shrimp or sauteed.
Speculative, indeed, I watch him
for a few more minutes and kiss
him on the forehead just like his
mother would do to me. Maybe:

it'll take him back to a time when
home was more than a home, a sense
to belong, a cognitive dream—a song.
I kiss him one more time, leaving
the house to meet friends at the park
for the Festivals Acadiens et Créoles.

Growing Up Lafayette

Gulf winds and nodded chimneys,
swimming in flooded roads, free,
the taste of mud—clay tapped our
tongues, gritted and coarse from
earth's burnt gumbo. Fais do do
lullabies sung from Sunday AM
at Randol's, we hummed along
and jumped on trampolines: up—
toward a Cajun soleil, drenched
shirts bought from Judice Inn,
a well-behaved lunch and two
bags of Zapp's Crawtators led
to evening naps. Come night—
howling mosquitoes: thick Creole
tomatoes, vined and curled, moon
filled eyes await another rain,
toujours—a rabbit and raccoon
play along fence lines and bark:
a scratch and a scratch, pressed
gardens, imprinted with souls
and soles of Deep South folk.

Nod to Juvie

Juvie! wut it do wut it b
tell me whatcha c.
cash.

money,

400 degree——z
round me B. we b
pay'n pennies @ da dollah menu,
price gone ↑ 10 peace venue,
↑ a quarta dats a hard sell:

holdinupdalineIholla dey can go 2 hell. loud
pipes while I dine.
big rims = mine.

        Juvie!

Da Gr8!

4eva Nolia.
sip sum Dew
foSoulja
Slim R.I.P.—lets take it slo
on tires. slo-mo w/ BBQ sauces, 🔥.
slidin with 🐤man—my CMB attire.

Ha!

Wear u @ Juvie—
trunk bounce mixtape $$:

Big Tymers Mannie Fresh I'm xcited

—nxt drive thru trip windows ↓ Run 4it rewound & hit ▶:

Beaucoup shake da head
            like hat flip take.

make da pawn trade da rook kiss da chef kiss da cook,

        Juvie! wut it do what it b
        tell me whatcha seeeeee.

Mullet Memories

Catfish tails strung like fresh laundry drying outside under splashes of the sun—a fried kitchen full of popping grease and crumbs, knives and cooks and chives and weathered pans made from blisters and callouses of familial traditions. Closed, and one game of bourre, glass ashtrays and leftover boudin—dawn reminds us that there's still another day. On my way home, I think about a bucket of marigolds and my Dadu sitting cross-legged in front of his prayer wall—cloths and water and tin cups: in his white dhoti soft and wrinkled. I'd peer through the door, pushing the curtain aside, and watch him, a ritual of my own, and always, from the balcony, the scent of washed clothes echoes through my nostrils. Maybe, a dog barking could be heard—maybe, a blackbird. In his own kitchen, a sizzling, sounding like sparks of an engine: aloo bhaji and mullet, bhat and butter, and when my grandfather is ready—after he has prayed, he comes and sits with me at the dinner table to play a game of cards.

Louisiana Longitudes and Latitudes

Hub City Diner—bread pudding
and chocolate malts after a plate
of red beans and rice: my friends,
a variety of Indians from their
mother's land, first generation
or second. A moment in our
laughter—a full restaurant,
regulars and strangers, unsure
where we belonged: a moment
in that laughter, with ketchup
bottles and Tabasco in front
of us: scraped plates and forks
covered in syrup, licked spoons
—I wondered if the owner thought
ever if this little spot in the Oil
Center of the Cajun heartland
would host and comfort, provide
an identity for young Brown folk
from across the oceanic latitudes
—longitudes, forgetting a longing.

The Bed of Spanish Lake

Cardboard boats and guitar-strung
fishing poles: duct tape sealed,
we were built for dreams, minnows
made for the catch of the day—
frogs laughed at our splendor. Moss-
lit sun, red-skinned clavicles, an oar
stolen from the neighbor's porch,
a pinky swear to return it the next
morning with a wind chime ditched
on the dirt road as a lagniappe gift.
We ran into the kitchen to show Ma
our jewels, shining—from Spanish
Lake, she clapped, and we brushed
our teeth and washed our necks:
dinner—catfish and red beans and rice.
Out in the cooler in the backyard, one
minnow for a future supper: years
from now when me and my brother
reunite for another reason at the house.

Twirling Dandelions

Green and yellow—a sparked field
where we taped four-leaf clovers
together, forgetting the meaning
of living at home and pondering
magical ways to steal ice cream
from the pink and purple and blue
truck coming around the turn—
we run with our hands together.
We run with pebbles in our palms,
asking for the cheapest cardboard
cups of vanilla with chocolate syrup.

We were royalty under the sun
—under the sun we were hidden
from shadowed jaws and crumbled
teeth. A melody to bounce in our
heads when the bed covers tore,
full of holes leading to our fears.
How one Sunday, with our faces
covered in swirls of amnesia,
I looked at you when no one else
was looking, knowing that once
upon a time in the future—past
rooster's crow and beyond wired
knotted fences, cut from our own
skin, we'll marry the moon's tongue.

Side by side, that tune hummed
from our breaths—through windows,
a fox darted to the pond to amuse
minnows, where we once fished
for stars after a reckoning, years
ago. Fingers clasped and puzzled:
in the bronzed straw plain, hearing
our childhood tremors sinking,
diminished—to taste sprinkles,
a past echo resting in our mouths.

Dhoti Blaze

mud splashed: teeth and truck,
a grind and growl—we watch
the world and rev the engine.
a spattered sky—churned air,
for a moment: a trip overseas,
time traveling to our childhood.
five sliced fish heads on a skillet
—sizzled scents and flickered
curtains of opened windows,
a distant conch mixed with caws
and barks: ma wipes her hands
on her sari and finds the salt
while we sit at the table playing
carrom with bhelpuri fingers.

reversed—covered in dirt,
walking into the kitchen
to prepare red beans and rice
while ma sits on the recliner
reading letters from our late
dadu. a window still opened
—a cow and a dog and a hen
find a flower in the patches
of puddled earth. my baro
bhai wipes his forehead,
a linen curtain flapping—
a memory of fresh dhotis,
washed and sun-dried, ma,
it's ready, we say. a pranam
and a hand—at the table,
just like then and just like
then: another game of carrom.

Bayou Bengali Recipe

Khichuri: let's make it Cajun—
add red cayenne beans and rice,
simmered in Mississippi River
delta. Let silt and marsh mound
before breaking it apart—hands
and nails to separate tributaries;
a spit to keep the Ganges hint
—from sipped waters a million
years ago, ancestral tongues
on a Sunday evening. Memories
are a must—closed eyes, raised
head to monsoon and hurricane.

Oh, needed, add sweetened sugar
cane as a light twist, to a stirring
past—an awakening stemming
from green peas and tomatoes,
lemon juice and ghee and a cup
of cinnamon. Daal—lunar moong,
a bitten carrot from a hare. Please,
understand, all cooked in a zydeco
accordion—and accordingly, sitar
moaned and plucked from fingers
of an auntie, dressed in sari; a rattle
of anklets upon taps of a pelican's
beak, eyes of swamp green moss.

Chandelier Palaces

Frozen: like back then when we held hands
during

Mardi Gras—Cajun Field, night:
loud—a chandelier palace.

The floats
already trickled

through, trumpets and beads

—like watching memories blurred into picture

frames, never hung on any wall. Carnivals
and carousels—cotton candy and teddy bears
made for dizzied heads. Live music on stage—
Cowboy Junkies and Wayne Toups echoed above
our voices. Your tiny black bag with thin straps,
full of tin cans

—we were too young then. Look
at us now, amid the past we hear cackles and crackles
while the horns distanced themselves from our tongues.

Two statues on the porch steps, a pup with a bent leg
and wise eyes—our hands still clasped like we never
moved.

Only the world kept its gravitation—us two
etched in the sky, between this star and that star:
        between those nervous seconds before the tangerine
        landed on my Chicago Bulls hat, I knew

what it meant to love freckles.

Glossary

Aloo: potato

Aloo Bhaji: fried potatoes

Amra: we

Amra tin jon natcham: we three once danced

Atmiya: relative

Baba: father

Bala: bangles

Baro bhai: older brother

Baro Dadu: eldest granduncle

Bhagavad Gita: scripture

Bhai: brother

Bhat: rice

Bhelpuri: Indian street food

Bindi: a small, round sticker worn on forehead

Bistirna Dupare: a Bengali folk song to the tune of "Ol' Man River"

Chingri Maach: prawn

Daal: lentils

Dajii: paternal grandfather

Dhoti: cloth worn by men that covers the lower body

Dida: maternal grandmother

Diwali: festival of lights

Doi: yogurt

Dosa: South Indian food, resembling a crepe

Eta: this

Ganga: Ganges

Gariahat: market area in South Kolkata

Ghee: butter

Goru: cow

Haa: yes
Khichuri: Indian food, made of rice and lentils
Kolkatar: of Kolkata
Koto: how much
Krishna: Hindu god
Luchi: fried Indian (Bengali) bread
Maach: fish
Mama: mother's brother
Masala: spice
Mashari: term used for mosquito nets
Mejo Dadu: second oldest granduncle
Moong: kind of lentil
Namaste: greeting
Oita: that
Pranam: a greeting of respect, bowing
Prithibi: world
Puja: prayer or worship
Raga: Indian classical music tune or melody style
Rickshaw: a form of transportation, by pulling a cart or carriage
Sangeet: music
Sari: a garment wrapped around the body, traditionally for women
Shona: dear
Sitar: Indian string instrument
Tala: rhythm in Indian classical music
Tandoori: seasoned chicken cooked in a clay oven
Thomani: paternal grandmother
Tumi kemon achho: how are you?
Tumi kothai: where are you?

Acknowledgments

"Us Cajun South Brown Folk" appeared in *The Emerson Review*; "Only The Cow Knew" and "Down Smede Road" appeared in *Susurrus*; "The Lost Saris Of Crawfish Season" appeared in *The Eunoia Review*; "Chandelier Palaces" and "Tiresias Up The Bayou" appeared in *The Wasteland Review*; "An Ocean Between Markets" and "Acadiana Rickshaws" appeared in *Prose Poems*; "Soft Marble Dirt" appeared in *Night Heron Barks*; "Soaked In Lightning" appeared in *Trampoline*; "Mel's Diner" appeared in *Red Ogre Review*; "A Day Dripped Day" appeared in *Cicada*; "Ladders" appeared in *South Broadway Ghost Society*; "The Dance Of The Wayfarer" appeared in *IceFloe*; "Just A Bit" appeared in *The Burning Hearth*; "A Slight Resonance And Reflection" appeared in *Claw & Blossom*; "Twirling Dandelions" appeared in *Stone Circle Review*; "An Evening Like Dawn" appeared in *Victory Flamingo Magazine*; "Morning Raga" appeared in *Journal Of Expressive Writing*; "Dhoti Blaze" appeared in *LEON Literary Review*; "Seasons Of The Mind" and "The Bed Of Spanish Lake" appeared in *Louisiana Literature*; "A Rabbit Under The Sun," "Kolkata Crawfish Claws," and "Two Dinner Tables" appeared in *The Chakkar*; "Abecedarian For The Sacred Roux" appeared in *Dust Poetry Magazine*; "Descendants" appeared in *Porch Literary Magazine*; "Mullet Memories" appeared in *Stanchion*; "Louisiana Longitudes And Latitudes" and "The Corner Table Of The World" appeared in *Where Meadows*; "Mist Over Meadow" and "Bayou Bengali Recipe" appeared in *Poetry South*; "A Louisiana Sestina" appeared in *New Verse Review*, "A Kolkatan Uncle Duplex" appeared in *MoonLit Getaway*; "Constellations: Broken French Bengali Broke English" appeared in *Ghudsavar*; "Mawmaw," "The Clasp Of The Rake," and "Growing Up Lafayette" appeared in *Columbia Journal*; "Nod To Juvie" appeared in *Full House Literary*.

Thank You

Cajun South Brown Folk couldn't have been written without the support, love, and care of the following lovely beings: Thank you to my friends, who without hesitation, have always shown so much kindness and support—your friendship means so much, truly and sincerely. Thank you, Mike Bourgeois and Andy LeGoullon. Thank you, Chad and Bianca Cosby. Thank you, Karl Schott and Mandy Migues. Thank you, Luke Sonnier. Thank you, Patrick O'Neil. Thank you, Jerome Moroux. Thank you, Ashleé Wilson. Thank you, Katie Culbert. Thank you, Story Frantzen and Jacob Camden. Thank you, Rien Fertel. Thank you, Sean Leon. Thank you, Casie Dodd. Thank you, Taylor Byas and Mona Lisa Saloy, for your thoughtful and kind words. Thank you, Catherine Fontenot for the cover art. Many thanks to all of the print and online journals for giving these stories a chance. Thank you, Lafayette Barnes & Noble and Cavalier House Books. Many thanks to the Literary Community who has provided so much encouragement. Thank you, Belle Point Press—for all of this. To my parents, Sarmistha and Subrata Dasgupta, my brother, Deep and my sister-in-law, Heidi—I love you all so much. Thank you, always, for being there. Love.

Shome Dasgupta is the author of *The Seagull and the Urn* (HarperCollins India), and most recently, the novels *The Muu-Antiques* (Malarkey Books) and *Tentacles Numbing* (Thirty West), a prose collection *Histories of Memories* (Belle Point Press), a short story collection *Atchafalaya Darling* (Belle Point Press), and a poetry collection *Iron Oxide* (Assure Press). His writing has appeared in *McSweeney's Internet Tendency*, *New Orleans Review*, *The Emerson Review*, *Jabberwock Review*, *American Book Review*, *Arkansas Review*, *Magma Poetry*, and elsewhere. He served as the the series editor for *The Wigleaf* Top 50 from 2019–2025. He lives in Lafayette, Louisiana, and can be found at www.shomedome.com and @shome_dasgupta.

Belle Point Press is a literary small press along the Arkansas-Oklahoma border. Our mission is simple: Stick around and read. Learn more at bellepointpress.com.

BELLE POINT PRESS